HOW TO STOP DOG BARKING

Methods to Stop Your Dog's Excessive Barking

Heather Hessler

CONTENTS

Title Page
Introduction ... 2
1 Understanding why your dog barks ... 4
2 Training Your Dog to Reduce Barking ... 13
3 Curbing the Instinct of Barking ... 19
4 Howling and Whining ... 26
5 Common Questions ... 31
6 Consistency and Patience in Training ... 35
7 Insights from Canine Behavior Experts ... 38
8 Creating a Harmonious Living Environment ... 40
CONCLUSION ... 42

HOW TO STOP DOG BARKING: Methods to Stop Your Dog's Excessive Barking

Heather Hessler

Copyright © 2024 Heather Hessler

All rights reserved.

INTRODUCTION

In "HOW TO STOP DOG BARKING: Methods to Stop Your Dog's Excessive Barking," readers will find a comprehensive guide to understanding and addressing their dog's barking behavior. Excessive barking can be a common issue among dogs, leading to frustration for owners and potential conflicts with neighbors. This eBook aims to provide practical methods and techniques to help dog owners effectively manage and reduce their pet's barking, creating a more peaceful environment for both the dog and its human companions.

The book begins by delving into the reasons behind why dogs bark excessively, exploring the various triggers that may lead to this behavior. By understanding the root causes of barking, readers can better address the issue in a targeted manner. From there, the eBook offers a range of proven strategies and training methods that can be implemented to curb excessive barking. These techniques are designed to be practical and easy to follow, making them accessible for dog owners of all experience levels. Throughout the eBook, readers will also learn about the importance of positive reinforcement in training their dogs. By using rewards and encouragement, rather than punishment, owners can effectively communicate with their pets and encourage desired behaviors. The book emphasizes the need for consistency and patience when implementing these training methods, highlighting that progress may take time but is achievable with dedication.

Additionally, "HOW TO STOP DOG BARKING" provides insights from experts in canine behavior and training, offering valuable perspectives on how to address barking issues effectively. By incorporating expert advice into the strategies outlined in the book, readers can benefit from a well-rounded approach to managing their dog's barking behavior. In conclusion, this eBook serves as a valuable resource for dog owners seeking practical solutions to address their pet's excessive barking. By providing a combination of insights into canine behavior, proven training methods, and expert advice, "HOW TO STOP DOG BARKING" equips readers with the knowledge and tools needed to create a harmonious living environment for both them and their furry companions. Enjoy your reading!

1 UNDERSTANDING WHY YOUR DOG BARKS

Barking is among the many forms of vocal communication for canines. People are often pleased that their dog barks, because it warns them of the approach of people to their home or it tells them there's something that the dog needs or wants. However, sometimes a dog's barking can be excessive. Because barking acts several functions, you must identify its cause and your dog's inspiration for barking before you can treat a barking issue.

Each kind of barking serves a unique function for a dog, and if he's repeatedly rewarded for his barking- in short, if it gets him what he wants -he can figure out how to use barking to his benefit. For instance, dogs who successfully bark for attention often pursue to bark for other things, like food, play and walks. Because of this, it's important to train your dog to be quiet on cue to help you stop his attention-related barking and teach him to complete another behavior instead -like sit or down -to obtain what he wants.

Many owners can determine why their dog is barking just by hearing that bark. For example, a dog's bark sounds different when he wishes to play compared to when he wants to come in from the yard. If you need to reduce your dog's barking, it's essential to determine why he's barking. It may need some time to teach your pooch to bark less. Regrettably, it's just not realistic to count on a quick fix or to expect that your dog will stop barking altogether. Your goal will be to decrease, instead of eliminating, the amount of barking. Keep in mind some dogs are more prone to barking than others. Additionally, some dog breeds are called "barkers," and it can be trickier to reduce barking in individuals of these breeds.

Why Dogs Bark

Territorial Barking

Dogs can bark exceedingly because of people, dogs or other animals within or getting close to their territories. Your dog's territory consists of the area surrounding his home and, eventually, anywhere he has explored or associates passionately with you: your vehicle, the road you take during walks and other places where he spends considerable time.

Alarm Barking

If your dog barks at any and every noise and sight no matter the context, he's most likely alarm barking. Dogs engaged in alarm barking normally have more rigid body language than dogs barking to greet, plus they often move, or pounce forward an inch or two with every bark. Alarm barking differs from territorial barking in that a dog might alarm bark at sight or sound in virtually any place at all, not merely when he's guarding familiar areas.

Attention-Seeking Barking

Some dogs bark at people or other pets to get attention or rewards, such as food, toys or play.

Greeting Barking

Your pooch might be barking in greeting if he barks when he sees people or other dogs and his body is relaxed, he's enthusiastic and his tail is wagging. Dogs who bark when greeting people or other animals could also whine.

Compulsive Barking

Some dogs bark exceedingly in a repetitive way, like a broken record. These dogs often move repeatedly too. For instance, a dog that is compulsively barking might run forward and backward along the fence in his yard or pace in his home.

Socially Facilitated Barking

Some dogs bark too much only once they hear other dogs barking. This sort of barking happens in the social context of hearing other dogs, even at a distance -such as dogs in the neighborhood.

Frustration-Induced Barking

Some dogs bark overly only when they're put into an aggravating situation, like when they can't access play pals or when they're confined or tied up so that their action is limited.

Other Issues That Induce Barking

Illness or Injury

Dogs sometimes bark because of pain or an agonizing condition. Before trying to resolve your dog's barking problem, please have your pet examined by a vet to eliminate medical causes.

Separation-Anxiety Barking

Excessive barking because of separation anxiety occurs only when a dog's caretaker is gone or when the dog is left alone. You'll typically see a minimum of one other separation anxiety symptom as well, such as pacing, destruction, elimination, depression or other signs of distress.

How to Handle Your Dog's Excessive Barking

The first task toward reducing your dog's barking is to figure out the kind of bark your dog is expressing. The following questions can guide you to precisely choose which type of barking your dog is doing to help you best address your dog's problem.

- When and where does the barking happen?
- Who or what is the focus of the barking?

- What triggers (people, object, situation) the barking?
- Why is your dog barking?

If It's Territorial Barking or Alarm Barking

Territorial behavior is frequently stimulated by both fear and anticipation of a perceived risk or threat. Because guarding territory is undoubtedly a high priority to them, many canines are highly motivated to bark once they detect the approach of strangers or animals near familiar places, such as their homes and yards.

This top level of motivation implies that when barking territorially, your dog might disregard uncomfortable or punishing responses from you, like scolding or yelling. Even if the barking itself is reduced by punishment, your dog's motivation to protect his territory will remain powerful, and he might try to control his territory differently, like biting unexpectedly.

Canines participate in territorial barking to alert others to the presence of unknown individuals or to frighten away intruders or both. A dog might bark when he sees or hears people coming over to the door, the mail carrier delivering the mail and the maintenance person examining the gas meter. He might also respond to the sights and sounds of people and dogs passing by your house.

Some dogs get particularly riled up when they're in the car and see people or dogs go by. You need to be able to judge from your dog's body posture and actions whether he's barking to say "Welcome, come on in!" or "Go away. You're not welcome here!"

To treat territorial barking, your dog's motivation must be reduced as well as his chances to defend his territory. To handle your dog's behavior, you'll need to block his capacity to see people and animals. Detachable plastic film or spray-based glass coatings can assist to obscure your dog's view of areas that he notices and guards from within your house.

Use secure, opaque fencing to encompass outside areas your pet can access. Don't allow your dog to greet folks at the front door, at your front yard gate or at your property boundary line. Rather, train him to go to another location, like a crate or a mat, and stay quiet until he's invited to greet properly.

Alarm barking is quite much like territorial barking in that it's triggered by sights and sounds. Nonetheless, dogs that alarm bark might do so because of things that surprise or upset them when they're not on familiar turf. For instance, a dog who barks territorially in response to the sight of unknown people drawing near will usually only do so when in his own home, yard or car. By comparison, a pooch who repeatedly alarm barks might vocalize when he sees or hears unknown people drawing near elsewhere, too.

"Quiet" Training

If your dog carries on alarm bark or bark territorially, despite your efforts to bar his exposure to sights and sounds that might set off his barking, try the following strategies:

Train your dog that when someone comes to the door or passes by your premises, he's allowed to bark until you say "Quiet." Let your dog bark three times. Then say "Quiet." Avoid yelling. Just say the command clearly and with ease. Then go to your pet, gently hold his muzzle closed with your hand and repeat "Quiet." Release your dog's muzzle, step away, and call him away from the door or window. Then ask him to sit and present him with a treat.

If he sits beside you and stays quiet, continue to keep giving him frequent goodies for an additional couple of minutes, until whatever triggered his barking has vanished. If your dog resumes barking instantly, repeat the above-mentioned sequence. Do the same outdoors if he barks at passersby when he's in the yard.

If you like not to hold your dog's muzzle or if doing so tends to frighten your dog or make him struggle, you can seek a different method. When your dog barks, approach him, smoothly say "Quiet," and then prompt his silence by giving him a steady flow of tiny, pea-sized treats. After enough practice of this sequence, over a couple of days or more of coaching, your dog will begin to determine what "Quiet" signifies.

You'll know that he's catching on if he regularly stops barking when he hears you say "Quiet." At this time, you can gradually prolong the time between the cue, "Quiet," and your dog's treat. Over several repetitions, progressively increase the time.

If the "Quiet" method is unproductive after 10 to 20 tries, then let your dog bark 3 to 4 times, calmly say "Quiet," and then right away produce a startling noise by shaking a set of keys or an empty soda can stuffed with pennies. If your dog is successfully startled by the sound, he'll stop barking.

The moment he does, call him away from the door or window, ask him to sit, and present him with a treat. If he stays besides you and stays quiet, carry on and give him regular treats for the next few minutes until whatever brought about his barking is gone. If he continues barking instantly, repeat the sequence.

If this process doesn't work after 10 to 20 attempts, seek professional help.

If your dog barks at people or other dogs during walks, draw attention away him with special treats, like chicken, cheese or hot dogs, before he starts to bark. Show your dog the doggie snacks by holding them in front of his nose and encourage him to nibble at them while he's walking past a person or dog who'd normally trigger him to bark. Some dogs do best if you ask them to sit as people or other dogs' pass. Other canines would rather move. Make sure you compliment and reward your dog with treats whenever he decides not to bark.

If your dog usually barks territorially in your vehicle, teach him to ride in a crate while in the car. Riding in a crate will limit your dog's view and decrease his motivation to bark. If crating your dog in your car isn't achievable, try having your dog wear a head halter inside the car instead.

To prepare your dog for times when real visitors arrive, ask friends who are acquainted with your dog to drop by randomly when you're home. Then ask other friends who don't know your dog well to drop by, too. With plenty of practice, your dog will be able to go to his spot and stay there, even when neither of you knows who is on the other side of the door.

Eventually, when real visitors come to your home, you can ask your dog to go to his spot as soon as they knock or ring the doorbell. After letting your visitors in, ask them to sit down. Wait about a minute before releasing your dog from his spot to greet them. You may put your dog on a leash if you think he might jump on your visitors or behave aggressively. After a minute or two of allowing your dog to greet people, ask him to lie down at your feet and stay. with something to keep him busy, if you repeat the ritual above for a while, your dog should learn to settle down calmly when guests visit your home.

Greeting Barking

In lieu of the "spot" training associated with visitors, dog owners should also learn and train their dogs about greeting barking. If your dog barks at people coming to the door, at people or dogs walking by your property, at people or dogs he sees on walks, his barking is accompanied by whining, tail wagging and other signs of friendliness, your dog is probably barking just to say "Hello.". He most likely barks the same way when family members come home.

Keep greetings low key. Train your dog to sit and stay when meeting people at the door so that he has something to do instead of barking. This will reduce his over excitement.

If your dog likes toys, keep a favorite toy near the front door and encourage him to pick up the toy before he greets you or your visitors. If he learns to hold a toy in his mouth, he'll be less inclined to bark. Although, he may still whine.

On walks, teach your dog that he can walk calmly past people and dogs without meeting them. To do this, distract your dog with special treats

Barking Types Chart
Types of Dog Barking
1. **Territorial Barking**:
    - **Sound**: Loud, continuous barking.
    - **Purpose**: To alert and protect their territory from perceived intruders.
2. **Attention-Seeking Barking**:
    - **Sound**: Persistent, often high-pitched.
    - **Purpose**: To get attention from their owner or other animals.
3. **Alarm Barking**:
    - **Sound**: Sudden, sharp barks.
    - **Purpose**: To alert to an unexpected event or sound.
4. **Fearful Barking**:
    - **Sound**: High-pitched, often accompanied by whining.
    - **Purpose**: To express fear or anxiety.
5. **Playful Barking**:
    - **Sound**: Short, repetitive barks.
    - **Purpose**: To invite play or show excitement.
6. **Compulsive Barking**:
    - **Sound**: Repetitive, often rhythmic.
    - **Purpose**: Often due to boredom or anxiety.
7. **Greeting Barking**:
    - **Sound**: Happy, welcoming barks.
    - **Purpose**: To greet people or other animals.

8. **Social Barking**:
    - **Sound**: Varied, depending on the context.
    - **Purpose**: To communicate with other dogs.

2 TRAINING YOUR DOG TO REDUCE BARKING

To reduce your dog's excessive barking, it helps to teach your dog a definite set of behaviors to do when visitors come into your home so that he has fewer chances to alarm bark. Additionally, when your dog performs his new behaviors and receives rewards, he'll learn that people coming into your home is a good thing.

Prior to training your dog to go to a spot and stay there when a door opens, you have to educate him how to "sit" or "lie down" and then how to "stay." After your pooch has learned these skills, your training to "spot" may begin.

Look for a specific place in your home where you'd like your pet to go when visitors come to the door. If possible, pick a spot that's at least eight feet away from the front door but still within your sight. It might be an area at the top of a set of stairs, inside the doorway of another room, your dog's crate, or a rug positioned at the far corner of an entryway.

State "Go to your spot," let him see his treat, and then throw the treat onto the spot where you'd like him to go and stay. Do this sequence 10 to 20 times. By the tenth time, pretend-throw the treat to make your dog begin to move toward the spot on his own. As soon as he's standing on his spot, throw him the treat. As he catches on, you can stop making the fake throwing action with your arm and just give him the command, "Go to your spot." Then wait until he does and reward him.

Once your dog is reliably going to his spot, change your position when you send him there. Practice cueing him to go to his spot from several angles and distances. For instance, say "Go to your spot" when you're standing just a couple of steps left of it. After a few repetitions, move a couple of steps to the right of the spot and say, "Go to your spot" from there. Then move to another part of the room, then another, and so on and so forth. In the end, practice standing by the front door and asking him to go to his spot, just as you might when guests arrive.

Once your dog masters going to his spot, start training him to sit or down when he gets there. As soon as your dog's rear end hits the floor on the spot, reward him with another (maybe a different) tasty treat. Then "give him another cue (you can use "Yes" or "Okay") and let him move off the spot. Execute these steps at least 10 times per training session.

Now, you may add stay into your exercise. Stand next to your dog's spot. Ask him to sit or lie down, say "Stay" and wait for a second. When he executed your command, praise him with a cue word and give him a treat. After you deliver the treat, say "Okay" to release your dog from the stay and motivate him to get off the spot. Do this sequence at least 10 times every training session.

Progressively increase from one second to several seconds but change the time so that sometimes you make the exercise easy (a shorter stay) and on other occasions, you make it hard (a longer stay). If your pooch starts to get up before you say your affirmative cue word, say "No" (or any cue word you'd like to represent 'no') and immediately ask him to sit or lie down on his spot again. Then make the exercise a little easier the next few times by asking your dog to hold the stay for a shorter time. Steer clear of pushing your dog to accelerate the progress or testing him to see how long he can hold the stay before getting up. This practice just sets your dog up to fail.

Succeeding Steps with His Other 'Humans'

The next step in "Go to Your Spot" training is to recruit friends and family to help you conduct mock practice visits. Arrange to have someone come to the door. You will work with your dog to help him stay on his own.

Be prepared! This will likely take some time before he gets the drill. When you open the door, one of two things can happen.

- Scenario A: Sometimes you leave your dog there on his spot while you talk to the

person at the door, as if your visitor is a courier or delivery person. Your dog never

gets to say hello. (However, you, the person or both of you should frequently toss

treats to your dog to reward him for staying.)

- Scenario B: At other times, invite the visitor in. Wait until the person sits down

somewhere, and then release your dog to join you and your visitor.

When you have a friend help you with a mock visit, be sure to repeat the scenario over and over, at least 10 to 20 times. Practice makes perfect. With each repetition, it will become easier for him to do what you expect because he'll be less excited by the whole routine—especially when it's the same person at the door, repeatedly.

Continue to recruit people to help you practice "Go to Your Spot" exercises until your dog reliably goes to his spot and stays there until you release him with your cue word.

Steps to Take to Reduce Excessive Dog Barking

One reason that it's so easy to live with canines is that they are one of the most expressive creatures in the world. They find a way to let their humans know what they need. Although, they often do this by barking or whining. It's not pretty, however, when your dog barks to demand anything and everything, needed or not. This pattern of barking does not happen by accident. A demanding, noisy dog has been taught to be this way (normally, not in purpose). To get your dog to stop, you'll need to consistently not reward him for barking. Don't try to figure out exactly why he's barking. Ignore him instead.

Treatment for this kind of barking can be tough because, most of the time, pet parents unwittingly reinforce the behavior—sometimes just with eye contact, touching, scolding or talking to their dogs. To canines, all of these human behaviors can count as rewarding attention. Try to use crystal-clear body language to convey to him that his attention seeking barking is inappropriate and going to fail.

To achieve this, try your best to never reward your dog for barking at you again. Sometimes, it's easier to avoid problems by eliminating the things that cause your dog to bark. If your dog barks to ask you to retrieve his toys from under the sofa, block the space so that the toys don't get stuck beyond his reach. If your dog barks at you when you're talking on the telephone or working on the computer, give him a tasty chew bone to occupy him before he starts to bark.

Compulsive Barking

Dogs occasionally become compulsive barkers, meaning they bark in situations that aren't considered normal or they bark in a repetitive, fixed or rigid way. If your dog barks repeatedly for long periods of time, apparently at nothing or at things that wouldn't bother other dogs, such as shadows, light flashes, mirrors, open doors, the sky, etc., you may have a compulsive barker.

If your dog also does other repetitive behaviors like spinning, circling or jumping while barking, he may be a compulsive barker. To help reduce compulsive barking, you can try changing how you confine your dog. For instance, if your dog is tied or tethered, you can switch to keeping him loose in a safe fenced area, or if he's left alone for long periods of time, you should increase exercise, mental stimulation and social contact.

Anti-Bark Collars

A variety of devices are designed to teach dogs to curtail

barking. Most often, these are collars that deliver an unpleasant stimulus when your dog barks. The stimulus might be a loud noise, an ultrasonic noise, and a spray of citronella mist or a brief electric shock. The collars that make noise are ineffective with most dogs. One study found that the citronella collar was at least as effective for eliminating barking as the electronic collar and was viewed more positively by owners.

Virtually all dogs become "collar-wise," meaning that they learn not to bark while wearing their anti-bark collars but revert to barking when they're not wearing them. Collars that work on a microphone system to pick up the sound of a dog's bark should not be used in a home with more than one dog because any bark from a dog can activate the collar.

Anti-bark collars are punishment devices and are not recommended as a first choice for dealing with a barking problem. This is especially true for barking that's motivated by fear, anxiety or compulsion. Before using an anti-bark collar, seek the help of your vet.

What NOT to Do

Do not encourage your dog to bark at sounds, such as pedestrians or dogs passing by your home, birds outside the window, children playing in the street and car doors slamming, by saying "Who's there?" or getting up and looking out the windows.

Do not punish your dog for barking at certain sounds, like car doors slamming and kids playing in the street, but then encourage him to bark at other sounds, like people at the door. You must be consistent.

Unless a veterinary behaviorist advises you to do otherwise, never use punishment procedures if your dog is barking out of fear or anxiety. This could make him feel worse and, as a result, his barking might increase.

Never use a muzzle to keep your dog quiet for long periods of time or when you're not actively supervising him. Dogs can't eat, drink or pant to cool themselves while wearing muzzles, so making your dog wear one for long periods of time would be inhumane.

Never tie your dog's muzzle closed with rope, cord, rubber bands or anything else. Doing this is dangerous, painful and inhumane.

3 CURBING THE INSTINCT OF BARKING

Barking is a natural form of canine communication. As with many behavior problems, sometimes natural instincts develop into unacceptable behavior.

To curb the instinct, you must determine why your dog is barking. This chapter will provide help to determine the root of behavioral barking.

- Nuisance barking. The primary reason for nuisance barking is to get your attention. This behavior interrupts meals, phone calls, and quiet leisure time. Seemingly, your dog is bored and desires some stimulation.
- Remove the cause and effect. If your dog barks to command you, don't respond. If your dog barks at you and you pick up the ball and play fetch, your dog has now trained you.
- Change the pattern. If your dog barks at you, perform three to five minutes of obedience commands, and then (if your dog cooperates) play.
- The harder your dog tries to make a certain point, the further away she should be from achieving the goal. Repeated barking should be met with removal from the social situation (crated).
- One of the easiest ways to correct nuisance barking when your dog isn't under leash control is a bark collar. Bark collars administer an automatic correction when your dog barks. As with remote collars, bark collars come

in a variety of styles and should be properly researched before purchasing. Bark collars should only be used with nuisance-related barking. Using a bark collar for stress-related barking or threat barking may make the problem worse.

- Threat barking. All dogs have basic territorial instincts, stronger in some breeds than others. Barking usually stops after the threat is taken away. Boundary agitation can strengthen the response intensity and is typically a contributor to uncontrolled threat barking. Remove boundaries for boundary agitation.
- You probably will have an easier chance at changing the color of your dog's fur before you can extinguish a truly territorial dogs' bark. But with proper conditioning, your dog should stop barking after the leader says enough! When your dog barks (and there is a reason to bark), praise him for the initial response. Next, tell him to "sit" to create a new thought path. If your dog continues to bark, correct with "no" and cue him with "quiet" and "sit." Praise as soon as your dog stops barking. Timing is crucial. Catch your dog on the first bark.
- Remove the visual stimulus. Prevent your dog from "patrolling" your house. If your dog insists on pacing from room to room, tether or post him with obedience commands.
- Reduce the intensity of the territorial response by counter-conditioning the boundary/agitation aspect of the behavior problem.
- Stress-related barking. Stress-related barking is triggered by a visual or noise stimulus that causes an anxiety response and barking. How can we tell stress barking from territorial barking? Stress-related barking will not stop once the stimulus has passed because the resulting stress remains in the dog.
- Most stress-related barking starts as simple territorial barking. Not knowing how to properly address

the barking, the owners introduce a negative stimulus like yelling, penny cans, bark collars, or spray bottles. The negative stimulus of the "quick fix" gradually attaches a negative emotional response with the territorial instinct, thus creating the barking.

- To address stress barking properly, you will have to address both the threat-barking response along with counterconditioning to the trigger. The counter conditioning should be done when a real territorial threat (e.g., visitor) is not present. A strong foundation as a leader will be essential for your dog to defer to your redirection.

When Barking Becomes a Nuisance

Barking is a natural way for dogs to express themselves -- it's a component of their language. Nobody would ever dream of "training away" or "punishing away" a feline that meows or a horse that whinnies. However, many people think that dogs shouldn't be permitted to bark or growl. First of all, you must realize and accept that dogs also have a language, and that a part of that language is to produce sounds. It's as simple as that. But considering that, it must be admitted that vocal expressions in dogs can produce powerful dimensions and can be an issue for their surroundings including the people in the neighborhood.

The main element to obtaining a solution to this is to learn to identify the point where barking has become exaggerated due to a need for attention, stress, or has changed into a "yelling" because no one listened when the dog tried to "talk" in a more normal way. It may happen in an isolated situation, or it may be chronic. But in either case, if you have stress involved, it often comes out through the mouth.

No matter what the cause is, you can do something about it. You must find the reason for the problem, what kind of barking you are confronted with, and understand the circumstances around it. Then you can identify ways to minimize the barking, remove whatever caused it, and in that way, get control of the problem.

The aim should not be to stop all barking for good. You should not be trying to take away from dogs the language they naturally have. The goal should be to get it down to a level and intensity that you can live with and that permits the dog to act in a way that is natural to him. And, of course, you need to look at your own reactions to a particular barking event since you may be overreacting.

Barking Frequency Graph
Table

Situation	Frequency (Barks per Minute)
Alone	5
With Visitors	15
During Walks	10
At Night	8
When Hungry	12
When Playing	20

This table represents a general idea of how often a dog might bark in various situations. The actual frequency can vary depending on the dog's breed, temperament, and training.

Increased Vocalization in Dogs

Troublesome Crying, Whimpering and Barking:

Substantial vocalization means unmanageable, excessive barking, whining or crying, often occurring at inappropriate times of the night or day. Such vocalization may be because of pain, illness, cognitive dysfunction syndrome (CDS), or could be associated with a decline in hearing in senior pets.

CDS is frequently linked to night waking, during which excessive vocalization takes place. Dogs that are bred for work and high energy activities may be susceptible to excess barking.

Excessive barking can also be related to behavioral conditions, which may be managed by behavior modification training.

Additionally, there are some breeds that are more well-known for excessive and inappropriate barking. Many breeds of terrier, like the Yorkshire and Silky terriers, are inclined to barking without cause and may make the most of behavioral modification training.

Indicators and Types:

Night vocalizations in senior dogs:
- Excessive barking in working-breed dogs
- Excessive barking in high energy, nervous dogs
- Vocalization brought on by pain or illness
- Vocalization troublesome to owners or others (neighbors)

Triggers:
- Health-related: disease, pain, CDS
- Anxiety or conflict
- Alarm barking - because of novel stimuli
- Territorial - warning or guarding reaction to sounds from outdoors
- Social or attention-seeking behavior that is bolstered by verbal commands or return of
   owner to room
- Distress vocalization (like howling or whining) - usually because of separation from
   mother, family, social group or owner
- Growling may be linked to antagonistic displays
- Stereotypical behaviors or compulsive disorders
- Breed - genetic characteristics

Diagnosis:

If your dog's increased vocalization is unusual, you will need to have health problems eliminated before considering behavior modification. The vet can perform a full medical work-up, including a chemical blood profile, complete blood count, urinalysis and electrolyte panel, plus a complete physical exam. Possible incidents that may have led to this situation are likewise considered, and a complete history of your dog's behavioral health prior to the symptoms will be considered.

It is important to rule out a non-behavioral, physical reason behind the vocalization first. Imaging can be useful for ruling out medical/neurological disorders.

Treatment:

A strategy must be developed which is personalized to suit your dog and your personal living situations, your household, and the sort of problem, being sure to try and resolve the underlying cause before behavioral modifications will begin.

Don't reinforce the vocalization. This consists of punishing the behavior, which is still considered to be attention. Instead, favorably reward your dog when he is calm and quiet and lead by example by remaining calm too. Also, counter-condition your dog to calm down when stimulated. Training your dog to be quiet on command will be the priority.

To stop your dog from becoming familiar with the attention received by barking or crying, a quiet response can be reinforced using head halters, bark-activated alarms, bark-activated citronella collars, and disruptive devices such as alarms or water sprayers. Another way that's been used to some success is to desensitize the dog to the outside stimuli using food treats until the response threshold is very high. Becoming more tuned into the triggers that induce your dog to bark excessively will assist you to distract your dog before he becomes excited or anxious.

Medications may be advised if there's real anxiety, discord, excessive responsiveness to stimuli or a compulsive disorder.

Management:

The dog must be brought back to the vet or to a behavior specialist to change the program according to your dog's particular response. Obedience training, head halter training and quiet command training are often effective in dogs. Dogs should be habituated and socialized to a variety of stimuli and environments throughout development, including to other people and pets. This desensitizes the animal to novel experiences, reducing anxiety, and over-excitation.

4 HOWLING AND WHINING

Howling is one of many forms of vocal communication used by dogs and has a direct connection to barking. Just barking, dogs howl to get noticed, to get hold of others and to announce their presence. Some dogs also howl because of high-pitched sounds, like emergency vehicle sirens or musical instruments.

Howling

Issues to Rule-Out First

Separation Anxiety Howling

If your neighbors call you and tell you that your dog is howling when you are at work, your dog's extreme howling may be brought on by separation anxiety. Separation anxiety howling only takes place when a dog is left alone or else separated from his human. This type of howling is usually coupled with at least one other characteristic of separation anxiety, like pacing, destruction, elimination, depression.

Health-related Causes

Dogs sometimes howl when they're injured or unwell. If your dog starts howling or howls more than ever before, take him to a vet to eliminate sickness and injury prior to doing other things.

How to Handle Excessive Howling

Howling in Responds to Sounds

If your dog howls because of some kind of trigger, such as

another dog howling or a nearby siren, he'll most likely stop when the sound stops. This kind of howling usually isn't excessive - unless, of course, the triggers happen often. If they do, you should use desensitization and counterconditioning to aid your dog learn to be quiet.

Systematic Desensitization and Counterconditioning

When the issue is rooted in how a dog feels with regards to a particular thing, often it isn't enough to just teach him a different behavior -like fetching a toy rather than howling, for instance. Instead, it's best to alter his motivation and feelings, which are the fundamental reasons for the behavior issue in the first place.

Systematic desensitization and counterconditioning are two typical treatments for fears, anxiety, phobias and aggression - basically any behavior problem which involves arousal or emotions. It's often most reliable to use these two methods together when trying to solve animal behavior problems.

Some dogs discover howling can get them attention from people. If your dog howls because of this, his howling will often occur in your presence when he wants attention, food or desired objects. If your dog howls to obtain your attention or "ask" you for things he wants, like food or toys, you must teach him a couple of things to be successful in curbing his behavior.

For starters, he must learn that howling doesn't work. Secondly, he also must learn that being quiet will work. If your dog understands that howling makes him invisible to you and being quiet earns him your attention as well as all the great stuff he wants, he'll quickly figure out how to curb his vocal behavior.

Disregard your Dog's Attention-Seeking Howling

To prevent accidentally rewarding your dog when he howls, completely ignore him as soon as he starts making noise. Don't look at him, touch him or speak to him. Don't try to scold him either. Dogs, like kids, often find any attention rewarding -even if it's negative one. So, scolding your dog might make his howling behavior worse. Just pretend your pet is invisible. If you find it hard to get this done, try folding your arms across your chest and avoiding him completely.

Reward your Dog for being Quiet

It's very easy to forget to focus on your dog when he's being quiet. If you want your pet to learn to stop howling for attention, you'll have to reward quiet behavior. At random give your dog treats and attention when he isn't making noise. It's also advisable to make and adhere to a new rule: Your pet doesn't get anything he wants (food, toys, access to the outdoors, treats, petting, etc.) until he's been quiet for a minimum of five seconds. If your dog howls to get your attention, ignore him until he's quiet, as described above. Then, after a few seconds of silence, you can focus on him again.

Finding Help

Because howling issues can be tough to work with, don't think twice about enlisting the help of a professional.

Whining

Whining is yet again, one of the many forms of dog vocal communication and has a close connection with barking. Dogs most often whine when they're seeking attention, when they're excited, when they're anxious or when they're trying to appease you.

Why Do Dogs Whine?

Appeasement Actions

Some dogs whine exceedingly when interacting with people and other dogs, usually while adopting a submissive posture.

Greeting Behavior

Some dogs whine during greetings. This sort of vocalization is usually stimulated by excitement and may be inclined to dogs or people.

Seeking Attention

Some dogs whine in the presence of their owners to get their attention, rewards or desired objects.

Anxiety

Some dogs whine because of stressful situations. In this context, whining at times seems involuntary.

Other Issues That May Cause Whining

Separation Anxiety

If your dog only whines right before you leave or during your absence, he may have separation anxiety.

Injury or Medical Condition

Dogs often whine in response to pain or an agonizing condition. If you notice that your dog vocalizes often or has suddenly begun to vocalize, it's vital that you take her to the vet to rule out medical causes.

How to Handle Excessive Whining

Appeasement Whining

Dogs can try to appease people or other dogs when they perceive a threat or aggression being directed at them. Appeasement behaviors include holding the ears back, tucking the tail, crouching or rolling over on the back, avoiding eye contact or turning the body sideways to the perceived threat. Appeasement whining is also a normal canine behavior.

You may be able to reduce your dog's appeasement whining by building her confidence. Try taking her to an obedience class that uses reward-based training techniques. You and your dog can also try trick-training classes or dog sports like agility, fly ball and musical freestyle. Playing fun, interactive games with your dog, like tug and fetch, can increase your dog's confidence. Avoid physical and verbal punishment.

Whining During Greetings

If your dog whines when greeting people, you can divert his attention to his favorite toys. Simply telling your dog to be quiet during greetings usually isn't effective because, unless you've taken specific steps to train your dog what the word "Quiet" means, he won't understand you.

Furthermore, most dogs whine when greeting people because they're excited, and in an incredibly aroused state, they may not have control over their behavior. Instead, use management procedures to help prevent your pooch from becoming overly excited.

Anxious Whining

Whining because of anxiety is difficult to eliminate unless the cause of anxiety is removed. Anxious whining is usually accompanied by other nervous behaviors, such as pacing, circling and licking. Many anxious dogs do not seem able to control their whining when under extreme stress.

Some medications may help reduce your dog's anxiety. Consult your pet doctor or a board-certified veterinary behaviorist to learn more about anti-anxiety medications. Do not give your dog any kind of medication for a behavior problem unless directed to do so by a veterinarian.

Steps to Avoid Whining

In addition to not reinforcing whining behavior, you need to reward your dog for being quiet. Teach your dog that she must always be quiet before receiving your attention, play or treats. Regularly seek out your dog to give her attention and rewards when she's not whining. When your dog understands that silence works well to get your attention, she won't feel as motivated to whine.

Don't hesitate to contact a professional in your area. Many pros offer group or private classes that can give you and your dog lots of great skills to learn and games to play that will reduce her appeasement whining, whining during greetings and attention-seeking whining.

5 COMMON QUESTIONS

My dog is barking excessively – what can I do?

Dogs bark excessively for numerous reasons including boredom, excitement, distress, territorial defense and fear and anxiety. Therefore, the solutions to problem barking differ from one dog to the next.

In the first instance, it's highly recommended that you talk to your vet who can refer you to a veterinary behavioral specialist. Vet behavioralist can help to determine the underlying cause of the barking and then develop a tailor-made treatment plan for your dog.

Treatment usually involves behavioral modification training. In some rare cases the use of veterinary medications in combination with behavioral modification may be required. Behavior specialists tend to ask owners a lot of questions and may offer to come out to the house to observe your dog in its own environment to identify barking 'triggers'. Triggers may include seeing or hearing a person walking past or the neighbor's dog.

Training should be based on the principles of positive reinforcement. That is, reward 'good' behavior – when the dog is quiet give him food treat or a pat on the head and avoid rewarding 'unwanted' behavior – when the dog barks ignore the behavior. Training should not involve punishment which tends to exacerbate the barking problem.

My neighbor's dog is constantly barking and disturbing me. What

can I do?

Usually, problems with barking dogs can be resolved without resorting to police or courts. If you do eventually wind up in court, however, a judge will be more sympathetic if you first made at least some effort to work things out informally. Here are the steps to take when you're losing patience (or sleep) over a neighbor's noisy dog:

Ask your neighbor to keep the dog quiet. Sometimes owners are blissfully unaware that there's a problem. If the dog barks for hours every day -- but only when it's left alone -- the owner may not know that you're being driven crazy. If you can establish some rapport with the neighbor, try to agree on specific actions to alleviate the problem. After you agree on a plan, set a date to talk again in a couple of weeks.

Try mediation. Mediators are trained to listen to both sides, identify problems, keep everyone focused on the real issues, and suggest compromises. A mediator won't make a decision for you but will help you and your neighbor agree on a resolution. Many cities have community mediation groups which train volunteers to mediate disputes in their own neighborhoods.

Look up the law. In some places, barking dogs are covered by a specific state or local ordinance. If there's no law aimed specifically at dogs, a general nuisance or noise ordinance makes the owner responsible. And someone who allows a dog to bark after numerous warnings from police may be arrested for disturbing the peace.

Call the police if you think a criminal law is being violated. Summoning a police cruiser to a neighbor's house obviously will not improve your already-strained relations. But if nothing else works, and the relationship with your neighbor is shot anyway, give the police a try.

Should I use an anti-barking collar to treat my dog's barking problem?

There are some products on the market that are aimed at

preventing dogs from barking such as sound collars - emit a high-pitched sound when the dog barks-, electronic collars - deliver an electric shock to the dog when it barks - and citronella collars - spray the dog's face with citronella scent when it barks.

Majority of vets and professionals DON'T recommend the use of these devices to stop your dog barking for several reasons:

• This type of training is called 'punishment' as the dog is effectively punished by the collar

for every bark. Punishment, as a method of training, is often ineffective as dogs often do

not associate the punishment (the citronella spray, sound or shock) with the behavior.

• This type of behavioral modification does not tend to be successful because it fails to

address the underlying cause of the behavior. Dogs bark for many reasons: play, fear,

separation anxiety, environmental factors, and boredom. These devices will not

necessarily solve the underlying cause of the barking and will only temporarily mask the

problem.

• Sometimes it is appropriate for dogs to bark (e.g. as a means of communication) in which case the collar punishes them for normal behavior. Because the collar does not discriminate between problem barking and normal canine behavior, there is a potential for abuse if the collar is routinely left on for too long.

The treatment of nuisance behaviors such as excessive barking should begin by attempting to address the root cause of the problem. It is a good idea to see a veterinarian or animal behavioralist to assess nuisance behavior and provide advice on how best to address it.

What can I do if my dog has separation anxiety?

Dogs are highly social "pack" animals that prefer to live in groups. Separation anxiety is a common behavioral problem that occurs when the dog is separated from their "pack" which is usually represented by the owner's. Separation anxiety is characterized by signs of distress when affected animals are separated from an owner or family group to which the animal is highly attached. Behavioral responses may include destructiveness, house-soiling, excessive barking, digging or pacing, among other signs.

The goal of treatment is to teach the pet how to be calm and relaxed during the owner's absence. It involves changes in pet-owner interactions, changes in leaving and return protocols, decreasing the anxiety associated with owner departure, teaching the pet how to be left alone, environmental changes and management.

Owners should consult their veterinarian for advice. They can either help you directly or they may offer referral to a veterinary behavioral specialist.

6 CONSISTENCY AND PATIENCE IN TRAINING

Time Required for Progress

Training a dog to curb excessive barking requires time and patience. Progress in modifying behavior does not happen overnight; it is a gradual process that necessitates consistency and dedication from pet owners.

Each dog is unique, with varying temperaments and learning speeds. Therefore, the time required for progress may differ from one dog to another. Some dogs may respond quickly to training methods, while others may take longer to grasp the desired behaviors.

It is essential for pet owners to understand that training takes time and cannot be rushed. Consistent reinforcement of positive behaviors through rewards and encouragement is crucial for long-term success. By patiently repeating training exercises and providing positive feedback, dogs can gradually learn to associate quietness with rewards.

Pet owners should set realistic expectations regarding the timeline for progress. It is normal for dogs to exhibit setbacks or lapses in behavior during the training process. These challenges should be viewed as opportunities for further reinforcement and improvement rather than as failures.

Consistency in training routines plays a significant role in determining the time required for progress. By establishing clear expectations and maintaining a consistent approach, pet owners can help their dogs understand what is expected of them. This consistency fosters a sense of security and predictability for dogs, aiding in their learning process.

In conclusion, achieving progress in curbing excessive barking demands patience, consistency, and understanding of each dog's individual learning pace. By investing time and effort into training while maintaining realistic expectations, pet owners can effectively address barking issues while strengthening their bond with their furry companions.

Achieving Results with Dedication

When it comes to training a dog to curb excessive barking, achieving results requires unwavering dedication from pet owners. Consistency and patience are key components in the process of modifying behavior, as progress does not happen overnight. Each dog is unique, with varying temperaments and learning speeds, making it essential for pet owners to invest time and effort into training.

Setting realistic expectations regarding the timeline for progress is crucial. While some dogs may respond quickly to training methods, others may take longer to grasp the desired behaviors. It is important for pet owners to understand that training cannot be rushed and that setbacks or lapses in behavior are normal during the learning process.

Consistent reinforcement of positive behaviors through rewards and encouragement plays a significant role in achieving long-term success. By patiently repeating training exercises and providing positive feedback, dogs can gradually learn to associate quietness with rewards. This consistent approach fosters a sense of security and predictability for dogs, aiding in their learning process.

Pet owners should view challenges as opportunities for further reinforcement and improvement rather than failures. By maintaining a consistent training routine and investing time into the process, pet owners can effectively address barking issues while strengthening their bond with their furry companions. Dedication to the training process is essential for achieving lasting results and ensuring a harmonious relationship between pets and their owners.

Comparison Chart: Dog Training Methods for Excessive Barking Table

Training Method	Description	Pros	Cons
Positive Reinforcement	Rewarding the dog for desired behavior (e.g., treats, praise).	Builds a positive relationship, effective for long-term behavior change.	Requires consistency and patience, may take longer to see results.
Negative Punishment	Removing something the dog likes when they bark (e.g., ignoring them).	Helps the dog learn consequences, can be effective for attention-seeking barking.	Can be difficult to implement consistently, may cause frustration.
Desensitization	Gradually exposing the dog to the trigger in a controlled way.	Reduces fear and anxiety, effective for specific triggers.	Requires time and patience, may need professional guidance.
Counter-Conditioning	Changing the dog's emotional response to the trigger (e.g., pairing with treats).	Can be very effective, helps reduce fear and anxiety.	Requires consistency and patience, may need professional guidance.
Clicker Training	Using a clicker to mark desired behavior followed by a reward.	Clear communication, effective for precise behavior training.	Requires learning how to use the clicker properly, may take time to master.
Anti-Bark Collars	Devices that emit a sound, spray, or shock when the dog barks.	Immediate response, can be effective for some dogs.	Can cause fear or anxiety, may not address the underlying cause of barking.

This chart provides an overview of various methods used to train dogs to reduce excessive barking. Each method has its own advantages and disadvantages, so it's important to choose the one that best fits your dog's needs and temperament.

7 INSIGHTS FROM CANINE BEHAVIOR EXPERTS

Expert Perspectives on Addressing Barking Issues

When it comes to addressing barking issues in dogs, expert perspectives offer valuable insights that can guide pet owners in effectively modifying their pet's behavior. One key aspect highlighted by experts is the importance of understanding the underlying reasons for excessive barking. Dogs may bark due to various reasons such as boredom, anxiety, territorial behavior, or seeking attention. Identifying the root cause of barking is crucial in developing an appropriate training plan.

Experts emphasize the significance of positive reinforcement techniques in addressing barking problems. Rewarding desired behaviors with treats, praise, or playtime can help dogs associate quietness with positive outcomes. This approach not only encourages good behavior but also strengthens the bond between pets and their owners.

In addition to positive reinforcement, experts stress the need for consistency in training routines. Establishing clear expectations and maintaining a consistent approach can help dogs understand what is expected of them. Consistency fosters a sense of security and predictability for dogs, facilitating their learning process and reducing excessive barking over time.

Another important aspect highlighted by experts is the role of mental and physical stimulation in preventing excessive barking.

Providing dogs with regular exercise, interactive toys, and mental enrichment activities can help alleviate boredom and reduce the likelihood of incessant barking out of frustration or pent-up energy.

Furthermore, experts recommend seeking professional guidance if barking issues persist despite consistent training efforts. A certified dog trainer or behaviorist can assess the situation objectively, provide tailored advice, and offer specialized training techniques to address specific behavioral challenges effectively.

In conclusion, expert perspectives on addressing barking issues underscore the importance of understanding the root causes of excessive barking, utilizing positive reinforcement techniques, maintaining consistency in training routines, providing mental and physical stimulation, and seeking professional help when needed. By incorporating these insights into their approach, pet owners can effectively curb excessive barking while fostering a harmonious relationship with their canine companions.

8 CREATING A HARMONIOUS LIVING ENVIRONMENT

Implementing a Well-Rounded Approach

Implementing a well-rounded approach to creating a harmonious living environment for both pets and owners is essential for fostering a positive relationship and ensuring the well-being of all involved. This approach involves considering various factors that contribute to the overall quality of life for pets, including their physical, mental, and emotional needs.

One key aspect of this approach is providing a balanced diet tailored to meet the nutritional requirements of pets. Proper nutrition plays a crucial role in maintaining their health and vitality, supporting their immune system, and promoting overall well-being. Consulting with a veterinarian or pet nutritionist can help determine the best diet for each individual pet based on factors such as age, breed, activity level, and any specific health concerns.

In addition to nutrition, regular exercise is vital for keeping pets physically fit and mentally stimulated. Engaging in activities such as daily walks, playtime, or interactive games not only helps pets burn off excess energy but also strengthens the bond between pets and owners. Physical exercise contributes to reducing stress levels in pets and preventing behavioral issues related to boredom or pent-up energy.

Maintaining a clean and safe living environment is another

crucial aspect of implementing a well-rounded approach. Regular grooming, cleaning of living spaces, and providing comfortable resting areas contribute to the overall comfort and health of pets. Ensuring that pets always have access to fresh water and monitoring their behavior for any signs of discomfort or illness are essential practices in creating a harmonious living environment.

Furthermore, incorporating training routines that focus on positive reinforcement techniques can help shape desirable behaviors in pets while strengthening the human-animal bond. Consistency in training methods, clear communication with pets, and patience are key elements in effectively teaching new commands or addressing behavioral issues.

By implementing a holistic approach that considers nutrition, exercise, environmental factors, grooming practices, and training techniques, pet owners can create an optimal living environment that promotes the well-being of their furry companions while fostering a harmonious relationship based on trust, respect, and mutual understanding.

CONCLUSION

Don't forget, barking is natural. It's a vital means of communication for dogs. But at times
problems can develop. As the pack leader, it's your job to step up and control excessive
barking. Remember the following guidelines stop nuisance barking once and for all.

Fix dog problem behavior and follow through.

Command your dog to quit barking using a look, a sound, or a physical correction. But don't end there. Your dog may pause and then go back to what he was doing. Be patient and train him until he actually GETS it.

Stay calm when training and stopping your dog from excessive barking.

Constant barking can be aggravating; however, you won't be able to fix the dog behavior problem if you're frustrated. The truth is your dog will mirror your energy. If you're irritated, he will be, too. And barking is a great release for that frustrated energy. Take a moment to curb your own internal barking first.

Stop the barking by challenging your dog mentally and physically.

Excessive barking is often the result of pent-up energy. If this is the case, the solution is simple: release that energy in more productive ways.

And lastly, get professional help to stop dog barking.

When you brought this dog into your life, you made a

commitment to provide the care he needs. Prevent dog barking and other dog behavior problems by calling in a canine professional to help him cope with a behavior issue.

Printed in Dunstable, United Kingdom